Exploring the Heart, Awakening the Mind

By
Jeffrey H. Williams

Diamondback Consultants
Mitchellville MD

Exploring the Heart, Awakening the Mind

Copyright © 2007
By Jeffrey H. Williams

All rights reserved under International and Pan-American copyright conventions. No part of this book may be reproduced, stored in a retrieval system or transmitted in any form, electronic, mechanical, or by other means, without written permission of the author.

First Edition

Library of Congress
Cataloging in Publication Data

ISBN 978-0-9679415-1-6

Published by
Diamondback Consultants
11601 Chantilly Lane Mitchellville, MD 20721
301 352-6280
dcpoetry@mail.com

Printed by
Signature Book Printing, Inc
Gaithersburg, MD 20879
301 258-8353

Other available books by the author
When The Heart Speak
Selections From The Heart

Table of Contents

DEDICATION 6
INTRODUCTION 7
THAT NONE ARE LOST 8

VOWS UNBROKEN 9

   NO MATTER THE DESTINATION 10
   I COME TO YOU 11
   WHEN WAS 12
   VOWS UNBROKEN 13

MISSING YOU 15

   MISSING YOU 16
   NOT FAR AWAY 17
   MY EASY BLUSH 18
   SOLITARY CONFINEMENT 19
   WHAT IF… 20
   WHEN DREAMS FLOAT 22

PASSION IN PLAY 23

   GRAY STROKE 24
   DINING DELIGHT 25
   BEHIND THE OPEN DOOR 26
   INFUSION 27
   EARLY RISERS 28

A MATTER OF TRUST 29

   OPEN AND SHUT 30
   WINTER BREEZE 31
   IT HAD TO BE 32
   WRITTEN ON HER THIGHS 33
   A MATTER OF TRUST 34

A PART OF ME 35

- TRUST 35
- WORDS OF SILENCE 36
- ORDINARY THINGS 37
- YOUR HAND IN MINE 38

ISLAND FUN 39

- CARIBBEAN NIGHTS 40
- LIMIN' 41
- CARNIVAL 42

REFLECTIONS ON LOVE 43

- HEROES 44
- BORN INNOCENT 45
- BRUSHES WITH LOVE 46
- ON THE COUCH 48

SURVIVING THE PAIN 49

- GROWING PAINS 50
- BLIND FAITH 51
- WATCHIN' TIME 52
- LIFEGUARD 54
- AS I RISE 55
- AND STILL THE WATER COMES 56
- DESTINY'S DREAM 57

HISTORY LESSONS 59

- COLOR TRAIN 59
- SHADOW OF A MAN 60
- OPEN YOUR MIND 61
- HAIKU 62
- HAIKU FOR MY QUEEN 62
- FRUIT OF MY HAND 63
- WHAT TIME IS IT? 64
- LIVING THE DREAM 65
- FADING RIGHTS 66

A TIME TO REST 67
- ROLL CALL 68
- ANGEL IN YOUR HEART 69
- MIDDLE OF THE NIGHT 70
- FOREVER IN THE HEART 71
- IN THE DARKNESS OF THE MIND 72

FROM ABOVE 73
- EVENING PRAYER 73
- PRAYING HANDS 74
- EVENING STAR 75
- MY BEST FRIEND 76
- FORGIVE ME, PLEASE 77
- AGAINST ALL ODDS 78
- THIS CUP I CANNOT PASS 79
- IN THIS HOME 80

Dedication

God is guiding me through powerful new directions and creating more depth and insight in my writing. This allows me to explore new opportunities of life.

I thank Him for these opportunities and for blessing me with a loving family and caring friends. With their support, encouragement and love, my whispers in the wind are no longer heard only in the dusty attic of my mind.

Introduction

Exploration is an instinctive natural process of human behavior where we venture into our surrounding seeking the unknown and observing it with amazement, hope, and most times apprehension. Whatever the outcome, we grow from the experience.

Exploring the Heart, Awakening the Mind is my natural progress towards growth. This collection of poems delves into the human condition and provides the reader insight, a window into their own heart. It allows you to reclaim the innocence of an open mind, to examine honestly the foundation of your beliefs and feelings. Do not check your emotions at the door. You will need them as you relive the dignity and shame of humanity, the fragility and strength of love and the sorrow and joy of faith.

Once you begin this journey, I will touch you, explore you, delight you, and expose you to yourself. You may shout with disagreement or quietly nod in acceptance as my thoughts awaken your mind.

That None Are Lost

On the edges of consciousness
linger thoughts that may challenge
and change the course of life.

Let none be lost...

Capture and refine them into
words the world will admire.

Share your inspirations...

Cause others to touch
the greatness within.

Preserve the art of written thought...

Vows Unbroken

No Matter the Destination

Lately, I've thought about us a lot and
everything we've gone through the past year.
Although I am unsure of where this is going,
I know we cannot get there without each other.

I remember the BY days, those "Before You" days
when my life felt distant, like a course charted to no where,
a time when I tried so hard to please those before you,
make them happy, fit into their description of me—being defined
by what I could do for them not by what we could do together.

I know every day with me has not been easy, but think about it;
when have you ever felt this good about yourself, felt safe with
the person sharing your bed or felt so cherished that each moment
seems like an answered prayer.

Our life together is a gift that defines the "suppose to be" of
relationships. When you touch me, or just look at me, I am
overwhelmed by the love and respect imparted by your presence.
Even when we argue, they remain intact and unquestioned.

Please, don't be naïve and believe I would let you just walk away
from what we have. I won't; neither would you. We are soul
mates, challenged to maintain the honor deserving of this blessing,
therefore, no matter the destination we will leave a single set of
footprints in the sand.

I Come To You

When I look at you my heart grows warm,
I wonder why I'm blessed to have someone who makes me feel
so content and well respected.

In your eyes, I see my soul cared for by your essence,
I see my fears fade away as your hand caresses,
I see our lives lived as one: one God, one love, one breath.

I come to you clear in mind and with an opened heart,
to re-examine long-healed wounds and remember they are past,
to share the unexplored caverns of our souls
and continue building bridges that unite us on common ground.

I come to you with no pretense and little apprehension,
you encouraged me to exceed the expectations of my thoughts
and taught me to understand the importance of keeping you
informed, especially when I chart new directions and need your
compass to stay the course and guide us through the perils.

Before the common, I come to you confessing what God has taught,
He is first; you are second and I, as distant third, to love someone
as yourself is truly a life's test. I learned the gift of love must be
spoken as well as shown, to fully comprehend its strength.
It must be honored and protected, offered freely, not parceled out as
reward for fulfilling someone's wishes.

I come to you with no tales of "happiness ever after"
and ask you to share the unknown joy, hurt and sorrow
that builds a lasting bond. I have not all the answers,
too many questions yet unasked. Together, we can find success
and build a life on trust. I pledge to you, my honor and respect,
through good and bad, ill and health until our heartbeats rest.

When Was

When was the last time I…

really kissed you before rushing off to work,
or hand carried flowers to you at your office
or called you at midday just 'cause--
      I knew you needed to hear my voice?

When was the last time I…

left a "thinking of you" note in your briefcase,
or made dinner and cleaned the kitchen because I arrived first,
or greeted you at the door with your favorite robe and
      bathed you by candlelight?

When was the last time I…

gave thanks for having you in my life,
when was the last time I breathed…?

Vows Unbroken

While strolling through the countryside, I felt a humbling pride,
as the miracle of your togetherness was revealed with every stride.
I know your first encounter was more than accidental
because your mutual attraction was a bit too coincidental.
You forged your marriage with a pledge to love, honor and respect.
Just watching you attend each other, I know this vow was kept.

Today, you celebrate fifty years of memories formed by daily prayer.
Each year shaped with the kind of love nurtured through selfless care.
Each prayer laid on a firm foundation of serving God's desires first
which sometimes meant foregoing self to quench thy neighbor's thirst.

Life presents many miracles, of which some remain unsolved,
but the tenure of your marriage is a question easily solved.
Your lasting union was not created by viewing crystal balls
nor by slaying magic dragons behind the castle walls.
Your marriage was made in heaven with the love of God involved
and with your steadfast faith in him, most problems were resolved.

May God bless your golden anniversary with joy and happiness
and may all your future anniversaries be filled with His Holiness.

Missing You

Missing You

Last night, a yearning consumed
my body, tremors raced my heart
sending ripples through my essence,
holding hostage any hope of rest.

I delved the enlightenment
of my soul and found you

                missing…

Like a puzzle missing its final piece,
I laid dormant and
incomplete awaiting the touch
of your hand to awaken
my dreamless sleep
with your return.

Not Far Away

If you don't often hear, "I Love You" spoken from my lips,
If you don't often feel my presence within your life,
If you don't often see the sparkle in my eyes,

Then you haven't heard the thunder before the storm,
nor felt the rain knocking at your door,
nor seen the rainbow outside your window.

If you don't often feel my touch, nor hear my voice,
nor see my face,

then when was the last time you let the sun warm your body,
or the last time you listened to birds chirping in the morn,
or the last time you watched a sunrise?

My Easy Blush

My easy blush, not shyness brought, my desire to hold your warmth and find out, if once again, I can feel, the tenderness your eyes express.

My internal compass cannot direct this pathway I have chosen.

This leap of faith, this cautious step; don't let me fall too hard.

Pick me up and brush me off, reintroduce me to affection.

I want to feel desired, loved; I know that's much to ask.

Share with me what you can, moments, days or hours.

Give to me one small slice of your warrior's heart.

Show me that the warmth I feel does bring ecstasy imagined.

My easy blush, not shyness brought, I want this dream fulfilled.

Solitary Confinement

The quietness of my home no longer brings the pleasure I once sought.
Without the presence of your voice, my refuge is now my prison.
Although, I flood my home with music,
it does not drown the silence of your absence.
I try drying my eyes with reruns of *I Love Lucy*,
        but I don't, I love you,
                I miss you,
                      I need you. . .
                          in my arms,
                              beside me,
                                  inside me.
I read to soften the burden of your memory
but each word reminds me of all those things I left unspoken.
Even sleep denies me dreams without you within my touch.
I cannot escape...you transformed my essence into a partnership
of rapture and anguish that craves your return.

                Please, release me for a day,
                        an hour. . .
                even for a moment,
        when my thoughts are not of you.
    You fever me in such a way
        no thermometer may gauge,
no ice may cool.
Your absence chills so deeply,
a thousand blankets could not preserve my warmth
Only my heart remains unfrozen because
            it cradles the warmth of your love
                and shelters the fire we shall share.

What If...

What if the windows to my soul revealed my desire for his touch and this night he turned my fantasies into the reality that I sought.

What if my smile unveiled the ability of his voice to strengthen my conviction that tonight he is my choice.

What if he said that tonight his all was mine to savor and I could enjoy his pleasures without embarrassment or restrain...

...Would I trust him enough to let my inhibitions free?

...Would I surrender the intensity of my arousal and deliver to his hands the secrets of my grail?

What if his eyes divulged the truth that tonight, I was his alone and that the passion we would share would be like none before.

What if his lips tasted so sweet, brown sugar unrefined, and my tongue became uncontrolled as my thighs began to dine.

What if I began to shudder, when his kiss caressed my neck and slowly crossed my torso finally resting on my hip...

...Would I for one night let my body decide its pleasure and create lasting memories that one night can be forever?

...Would I wake from this dream feeling not quite alone, knowing that my lover's hand still rested on my soul?

What if for tonight I fell in love again, and gave without justifying the acceptance of my heart with the practicality of my mind.

What if at the climax of our evening, words were not enough and our eyes reflected the unforgettable love hearts could not pretend.

What if these moments were meant as brief encounters of our time, where the fullness of my heart rested, cradled safely in his care and my true essence surfaced through our honest sharing…

…Would my spirit be replenished and my faith be redefined by the spirit of the man who suspended my breath in time?

When Dreams Float

In the aftermath of despair lingers a glimmer of hope
that the heart will mend, the spirit will forgive and
the mind will remain open to the advent of love.

Who could have known that one dark night could make
day forget the stormy dawn of past misery and pain,
allowing the fullness of her light to recast his shadow
and overcome any thoughts of unfulfilled desire.

Who could have known that embracing her
in the sensual warmth of his evening breeze
would rejuvenate the joy of possibilities.

When dreams float,
a broken heart knows pain passes,
time heals and wisdom reaffirms
the soundness of commitment to self-love.

When dreams float,
two well-worn hearts find comfort by openly
exposing their wounds to explore their healing
and draw first light of the happiness they deserve.

When dreams float…love thrives.

Passion in Play

Gray Stroke

Gray hairs,

reminders of charcoal embers

and ash cooling in an evening breeze,

still warm enough to satisfy your midnight tease.

Dining Delight

Appealing appetizers adrift amongst adventurous
attitudes accelerate amorous appetites

Smooth skin suddenly senses subtle stroking
and silently surrenders to savor sensations

Enlightened eyes enjoy evoking erotic entrees
of endless evolutions of ecstasy

Tummies tighten as tongues tantalize
tender tasty finger tips

Limber limbs lavish in layers of love
sautéed in libations of lust

Handsome hands help healthy hips
harness body heated hormones

Bashful bodies now boldly burn
and bask beneath breathless basting

Cerebral calm after climactic crescendos
created by consensual consumption

Behind the Open Door

Soothing water caresses,
chestnut silhouette slow dances
behind steam frosted glass,
lavishing in lavender scent.

Undisturbed by another presence
readied with hungry towels to
swallow in terry cloth fluff...

Hands explore,
heart surrenders to parting lips,
fingers tease glistening treasures,
            rapture floods his hand,
      ancient pleasures succumb;
he tastes this offering of the chaste.

together reaching heightened pleasures,
yet, honor remains intact,
another candle lit.

Sultry shower, its cleansing power
too late to unseal their fate.
Soul mates found, love abounds
handwritten on their hearts.

Infusion

Simmering on a freshly made bed,
Chestnut and mocha lounge waiting for the boil,
catching up on yesterday's news,
not really hearing the words,
more enjoying the rhythm of the voice...
anticipating the boil.

Temperatures rise as thoughts succumb to
memories of earlier admissions.
No reason to hide, the tide has arrived,
bubbles begin forming
Bodies embrace, ending the chase,
cat and mouse need not be played.
Slowly imbibed, eyes hypnotized,
transfixed on love undisguised.

Rapture's grip held on the lips,
the pleasure seems never-ending,
Ecstasy's blush reddens the flush,
kettle now whistling amour,
The warmth of desire now fills the entire;
contractions surround all that is shared,
Sighs of relief, tender repeats of many evenings
the future will bare,
Sleep takes its stride, as minds rest their pride
and dream of what love has prepared.

Early Risers

Crisp winter air surrounds, like scavengers circling,
hoping to nip more than noses, foolish enough
to brave the frosty trek of a morning call.

Sunrise gently wakes
new lovers snuggly wrapped in flannel sheets,
simmering in the aftermath of another early morning rise.

Memories of last night still linger
as their lips surrender to another slow dance.
Ecstasy on the tip of her tongue, hmm hmm hmmmm, echoes…

Sunrise gently warms
new lovers peaceful resting as spoons in a drawer,
simmering in their dream of tomorrow's early morning rise.

A Matter of Trust

Open and Shut

Your "I heard you" has become an obstacle
to listening and understanding that meaningful
words do pass through my lips,

And your impatience locked on your need
to be right instead of our need to be whole,
disrupts any hope of comprehending what I said…

And that "rolling your eyes" attitude extinguishes
my desire to rebuild the foundation you so casually
tear down without contemplating the consequences…

Once again, you argue using classic aural oral inversion
Mouth opens, ears close…

Sometimes the truth hurts more than sticks and stones.

Winter Breeze

Although we made love many times before,
I sensed tonight a difference,
more urgent, as if time extinguished.

I remember lips tasting, engaging,
          savoring me, hopefully lost in reality,
Urging me to take all, anxiously
          slipping me further inside
and lavishing in the fullness.

While I slept, I felt you vanish,
I woke remembering your whisper…
"Don't fall in love with me."

It Had To Be

forgetting you, like forgetting to breathe,
easy as dancing on the head of a pin,
you became such a natural part of my life,
I could not imagine the magnitude of my emptiness
when you retreated to the secluded safety of your past
and pelted me with pebbles of regret landing like boulders
of anguish propelled with despair,
                      knowing it had to end…
                                      this way…

Written On Her Thighs

Deception spoiled the air; hesitation her stride
Her eyes told no lies;
another man's presence lay on her thighs.

Nipples too sensitive, body too drained,
the earlier man's essence boldly remained.

Her body betrays what he never spoke;
he noted another man's marks impeding his stroke.

Remorse never shone, "my body" her tone,
Her lips justified, old friends sharing past times.

He expressed no despise, showed no surprise,
He left her that night to mourn the sunrise.

Some things never spoken, some things cannot hide;
like the essence of another man written on her thighs,
like the presence of another man red in his eyes.

A Matter of Trust

Mornin', last night, incredible,
and that little thing I did that curled your toes...
that's right, you remember;
well Baby, hold that thought for a very long time
'cause there'll be no more, in fact there'll be no more of us.
It's a matter of trust.

Baby, what I did for you, I did because I thought you were special,
deserving of the best I offer. Deserving of the slow easy way
I made you feel, an intimacy precious and special to our relationship,
not for sharing outside of us.

Now your so-called girls ease up on me going, "psst, psst, ooooh
I heard whatcha did for my girl, can you hook me up?"

And do you really think our business in the streets builds trust,
and what's all this street talk about my nose being wide open.
Well I guess that's right, open enough to smell your scent fading
in my memory. I trust you catch my drift.

A Part of Me

Trust

The grace and honesty I see in your eyes are gifts with which few are blest.

Every time, I engage your eyes,

        I feel as though you read my soul

                and understand my vulnerabilities

yet confident that this knowledge will not be used to disarm.

Words of Silence

How does one share that last ounce of love,
that very small part which surrounds and protects your heart,
that little bit that defines self worth,
an unconditional belief that you are someone of value…
     to love,
       to listen to,
         to learn from.

How does one open to another,
the vulnerability of their soul,
the fragility of their heart,
the insanity of their mind without fear of utter and complete rejection…
Taking chances
and leaps of faith provide courage to young love to give that last ounce.
Experience and acceptance of faith afford mature love the knowledge
that love is shared, not given.

Although, we may lose opportunities to share,
few lose the capacity to love,
the mind is too complex to be driven mad,
the heart is too strong to break, the soul is everlasting,
a perpetual pool of rejuvenating energy,
just waiting to be shared so it may envelop and comfort the spirit.

How does one show, how does one share…
Sometimes listening is the greatest gift for sharing…showing love…

How does one share that oh so private happiness,
How does one show, how does one share,
it's not magic,
     it's just done
We lose the capacity to share, never the ability.

Ordinary Things

It is the little things I want to share, your ordinary, everyday things.
The so called insignificant that others tend to miss.
The everyday changes you do for you, your nails,
your hair style, or maybe just your walk,
those are the moments I want to share.
Fifty years from now, when I watch you from across a room,
I still want to smile and feel your warmth inside.

To watch the graying of your hair, the character etching
around your eyes, these are the pleasures that I seek.
To be there when you evolve to a greater aim
or work at something different and succeed at making change.
To watch you emerge from the caterpillar's cocoon,
transformed, renewed with the butterfly's dazzling swirl.

It is so important for me to know the changes in your life.
It may be the way you talk or write your name,
the way you see the world or focus on the plain.
That's why I revisit and share your passing days.

When I look at you tomorrow, I don't want to be surprised
because I failed to ask what changes did arise.
I want to look at you and be aware of the changes most won't see.
That's a responsibility that I will not leave to chance.

Today, I want to see the world through your eyes
and hear the birds through your ears.
Today, I want to walk the world wearing the loafers I helped select
because that is one true way our love will remain alive.

Your Hand in Mine

Walking on a sandy beach or down a crowded street,
your hand in mine, everything seems at peace.

Traveling awhile in silent repast, holding our thoughts
for careful unwrapping, precious gifts for us to bestow.

You touch my shoulder to slow my pace,
my arm surrounds your accepting waist, together we sigh relief.

We sit for a time, exchanging our past,
building a foundation in common.

Exposing our fears, exploring our hopes,
expectations of each to the other.

Your lips to my ear, the music of love,
expressing some hidden desire.

My eyes to your soul then grasping your heart,
sweetness found on your lips.

As evening begins, we find our way home,
answering the call of passion's love.

Time suspends, morning arrives,
we awake embraced by the sun.

Clearing my eyes, I find no surprise,
your hand still holding mine.

Island Fun

Caribbean Nights

Ocean waves, endless as the possibilities existing beyond
the horizon; forever escaping…
                      Seagulls suspended in air,
          floating effortlessly on invisible currents of faith.

Brilliant sunset slowly hides behind a never-ending
field of ocean blue. Worries fade as nighttime silhouettes
appear and calm overtakes the apprehension of doing nothing
…the reality of relaxation becomes the lesson of this evening.

Shades of midnight-blue sky play hide and seek with
stars and clouds reflecting in the peaks and
valleys of calming waters.

Gentle waves quietly rock sailing ships secured in
their slumber berths. Serenity surrounds the harbor's claim
granting safety from the unknown.
                Red and green lighted buoys stand guard
                            as moonlight
                        shadows late-night travelers
                                    illuminating their path
            to yesteryear's glory and tomorrow's rebirth.

Lovers hold hands and rub shoulders mesmerized
within each other's eyes; small-talk about sharing
pleasures without the pace of urban hustle.

Calypso and Reggae ride the breeze beckoning
newcomers and ol'timers to move
to the beat of Caribbean nights.

Limin'

Lounging and laughing
above fan-feed breezes coolin'
well-fed companions chillin' on Sunday afternoon.

Carib™ and Solo™ shared with traditional rum
loosen tongues in carefree conversations
solving world problems under the Caribbean sun.

Calypso and Steel Pan fill the ears of comfortable comrades limin' in
the kitchen, catchin' up on lifestyle changes,
loving the commonality of native tongues sharing
colorful phases of local thought insightful beyond the island shores.

Lounging and laughing
well-fed companions salute the island fun.

Carnival

Festive celebration of freedom's long fought victory
over colonized domination of souls too rich to remain
silent or stagnate in the guise of liberation.

Colorful blending of cultures and customs;
ancient civilizations redefined as one people
reflecting the diversity and unity of a nation.

Calypso, Steel Pan, Soca and Rapso converge in friendly
competition to surprise and satisfy the ingenuity of legends
and neophytes searching for authentic expression.

Cruisin' the panyards and fêtes, limin' with
foreigners and friends; teaching the newcomers
that some wine ain't for drinking nor subtle shaking.

Fleshy frenzy of fun-filled freed forms finally releasing
inhibitions trapped by societies preconditioning
of acceptable moral behavior.

Carib™ and Stag™ along with sweet Trini rum served with
Caribbean flair to lighten the load of playing Mas for two days
then chippin' into the twilight of las' lap tired and satisfied.

Pleasant memories of one fête too many or maybe too few,
rejuvenating at Maracas Bay or Pigeon Point with roti, pelau,
bake and shark, and curry crab and dumplings.

Carnival - A reminder that enjoying life is not age bound
but self bound if you choose, the inconvenience of getting old
as a reason not to relish God most precious gift…
                    …life in sweet, sweet T & T.

Reflections on Love

Who are the heroes; ordinary people, everyday folk, unassuming yet...giving

Heroes

Heroes do the extraordinary almost everyday,
by placing the welfare of others above their personal gain.

Healing with their hands, as their touch takes away my pain.
Educating with their experiences, as they teach how life may strain.
Reassuring with their faith, as they lead a Christian life.
Open with their hearts, as they understand my strife.
Everlasting with their love, as they sacrifice for my growth.
Sharing with their time, as they fulfill the Parents' Oath.

Heroes do the extraordinary almost everyday...
They are not fancy people; we meet them any time of day.

They do not score home runs or touchdowns in a way one may expect.
Their way of earning extra points is very subtle yet easy to detect.
They travel life's highway helping the stranded along the way,
without concern for potholes that lengthen their journey's day.
They stand out in a crowd not by a boisterous display,
but by the reassuring aura they confidently convey.
Heroes do not plan their lives around material gain.
They measure their success by relieving others' pain.
Most heroes meet the biggest challenge, the challenge of daily living,
by creating an atmosphere for discipline as well as selfless giving.

My heroes, my parents, my personal thanksgiving,
they are the extraordinary each and everyday.

Born Innocent

So little, so young, so innocent,
prodding and pushing their way through a grown-up world.
Too small to carry out tasks of serious consequence
yet too important to ignore.

Instant to tears over things they don't understand
and when they can't have their way.

Precious smiles full of giggles, honest laughter without pretense.

Ever demanding, demanding so much time,
giving love without exception,
feeling free of pain and fear whenever parents hold them near.

Running free with time to play, free to run, free to play,
free to stay...innocent.

Brushes with Love

She sat facing the mirror of her hand-carved vanity,
now spider-cracked along its edges and spotted with age,
as are her hands; each a reminder of their history.

A silver-backed hairbrush slowly glides through naturally
grayed hair. The brush, his wedding gift; he so enjoyed watching
her use it as he pretended to read from his leather recliner placed
just in sight of her vanity. This attention always brought an amusing
pleasure to her day.

Clad only in an ivory cotton dressing gown barely showing its age,
except for the new embroidery around the cuffs, she surrenders
to the reflection. Gradually, a smile emerges as she feels his eyes
caress her hair and shoulders; she inhales the unforgettable aroma
that is his alone and exhales a contented sigh.

Her reflection admires the Mother's ring on her right hand;
five flawless gems display the family legacy of their now grown
children. On her left, a commitment too seldom shared,
fifty round cut diamonds set in gold, each honoring a year of marriage.
Having it made almost sixteen years ago, he concealed it until last year,
their golden anniversary.

As she stares at his faded photograph, her eyes fill with tears,
"Has it been six months since we stood at Arlington and
said farewell?
   The crackle of the rifles still lingers in my mind
        and the lone bugler rings in my ears."

His flag, now encased in a triangle of oak,
hangs over the bedroom fireplace,
a silent reminder of family, friends and freedom.

"Today is our anniversary", she reminds the reflection of his recliner.
Closing her eyes, she continues brushing her hair and smiling as she
feels his eyes caress her hair and his lips brush her ear whispering,
"Next year, we will be together."

…she inhales that unforgettable aroma and exhales a contented sigh.

On The Couch

Summer's new found freedom quickly fades as they sit
on the couch. Television and radio hold hostage young and old
as advertisers try their luck. The world's progressive changes,
violence, greed and lust in full display, luring and tempting
with dangerous games.

Mesmerized, their concentration never seems to dim,
their eyes unwavering from the fantasies unfolding in their minds.
Hearing not a question asked and ignoring calls to lunch,
contented listening to tales and stories,
letting imagination fill the blanks.
I watch their expressions change as new scenes
register in their thoughts.
A bit of jealousy crosses mine, my innocence passed long ago.

We are fortunate; "couch potato" found new meaning in our home.
Each week, library books entertain our children
and we proudly watch as they sit reading on the couch.

Surviving the Pain

Growing Pains

Mister, Mister let them be,
Listen to my honest pleas,
Let my children stay with me.
Let my acorns grow to trees.

Why's your mind so diseased?
Why you whip 'til they bleed?
They've done nothing to displease.
They're your children, they're your seed.

Blind Faith

Why did you let him touch me like that?
You told me, I was too young to be touched like that.
I trusted you to protect me from people like that.
You said, I would lose a young man's respect,
if I let him touch me like that.

You were supposed to protect my innocence from harm
and from shame. Why mother, why, when you heard
me cry, why did you let father touch me, why?

Watchin' Time

Black man, black man watching the prison hourglass
as the sands of your dignity timelessly pass.
Next time be careful 'bout raising your voice,
only the man has the right to make that choice.
Don't you know, your body is 'bout to burn
so sing to the Lord, he will help your soul turn.

Black boy, black boy safe streets are not in your play,
hoodlums and addicts try pulling you their way.
Why is your rappin' so full of joy,
when talkin' 'bout guns like "five and dime" toys.
Education is power so discard your chrome-plated tool
and learn true power by staying in school.

Black children, black children raising children is an adult game
so temper your urges and stop being lame.
Young men respect the young ladies,
don't treat them as cravings for your misbehaving.
Young ladies don't worry about nursing a child,
keep your body in check, enjoy life for a while.

Black girl, black girl be weary of the lines young men lay,
most times they're just trying to get a touch of your play.
Someday a woman you will become,
wait for the man who makes your world sparkle and hum.
He'll keep you singing 'bout the beauty of the African world;
diamonds and gold from the great ebony pearl.

Black woman, black woman left not alone,
the ghost of your man still haunts your home.
Your tears created the river Nile
and now feed the starvings of his crying child.
Sharp pains are flowing through your head,
as you sadly envision the prison hourglass next to his bed.

Lifeguard

Overcast skies filled
with roaring thunder
ignite wind-swept ocean waves.

Ocean waves
exhaust their energy against the shore, catching
unsuspecting wanderers like frosty foam
spilling from a freshly tapped keg.

Seagulls fly in formation
searching for remnants
from last night's seafood feast.
Empty shells of horseshoe crabs
scattered throughout the sand; reminders
of nature's continuous cycle of replenishment.

Tired friends and family
gather in laughter,
sharing moments of renewal
seldom found in daily living.

The power of the ocean heals injured souls
wounded by city pressures.
Captivated minds recover
by aimless wandering through
the serenity of the ocean's roar.

As evening comes,
rejuvenation sets in,
rebirth assured;
rested hearts resurface
ready to meet the challenges of tomorrow's dawn.

As I Rise

I am the first breeze passing through the aroma of a Spring after-rain
no longer encumbered by your misconception of my self-worth.

I am a blazed trail sprouting new growth fertilized
by the wisdom of experience no longer needing
your approval to make my place in history.

I am withering stereotypes and blossoming choices
no longer hindered by your inability to accept
that equality is not necessarily equal.

I am the weaker sex only in your mind,
my survival is no longer dependent on yours,
don't you understand; I am your complement
not your competition, your confidante not your chattel.

Although I bear the pain for your existence,
you will no longer use me as the outlet for your rage.
I am a gift to be cherished not chastised, praised not hazed.

My presence in the universe is no longer defined
by the limits of your vocabulary,
I am too dynamic to contain and too prolific to explain.
If you cannot stand by my side, do not stand in my way.

Although, you may never understand my complexity
nor comprehend my diversity,
you will respect my rise above adversity.

Don't you understand; I will survive…I will survive.

And Still the Water Comes

Wind rushing in an open window, curtains feverishly billowing
   Rain splashing against the screen
      Thunder rumbling, voices screaming
         and still I watch; unmoved, unblinking, analyzing.

Droplets form on the sill, overflowing onto the wooden floor,
   snaking towards the ancient Persian rug, ruin imminent
      and still I watch; unfazed by the destruction that surrounds.

As I move to close the window, the storm intensifies, piercing
   the screen with flying debris, drenching me with rain,
the wind chills and still I watch; unconcerned.

My home shudders and shakes, the front door flies open;
rain and wind invade. Standing in the doorway, I challenge
them, demand cessation, laughter echoes from the darkened sky.

Outside, soaked; lightning strikes near my feet, I shake my arms
towards the heavens and call for this insanity to end,
again and again I bellow to no avail.

In abject resignation I kneel; with head bowed,
I stretch my palms skyward and whisper, "stop the rain".
Immediately, quiet surrounds me. The sun's warmth cascades
across my neck and shoulders; allowing my surrender to exhaustion.

I wake in drying clothes, the storm now watching me.
I open the window; the curtains capture the wind like sails of a ship.
Nothing has changed, except my perception of what I can do…

The water still comes, and I watch, smiling; mindful of how
I've changed.

Destiny's Dream

I am the dreams of my parents,
the prophecy of my ancestors
and the legacy of my descendants.

Education and environment shaped my wisdom.
As I grew in knowledge, I understood that to be, I only had to try,
that to succeed, I only needed self-belief and faith.

As I continue my climb to actualization, I know I am prepared,
capable and worthy of the obligations entrusted to my care.
I shall not falter nor feign for I am a blest child,
whose path is protected, whose principles are hallowed
and whose humility shall accept the rewards bestowed by
my ascension.

Each day, I give homage to those who sacrificed for me
by performing my part to accept and create change as a
conduit for improving society.

If the impressions left by my presence relieves one suffering,
cures one soul or eliminates one thought of evil then my success
will be judged not by the accumulation of personal wealth
but by the decency of my actions.

The tears shed by my ancestors will become the rivers
safely crossed by my descendants as prophecy and legacy
coalesce into the dreams I shall fulfill.

History Lessons

If my eyes could share the stories of the trials my feet have seen.
Then my voice would share the joys only my heart has heard.

Color Train

Lights or brights, almost full human rights
Basic brown, walk most parts of town
Sepia black, stay across the track

Ignorance can be removed from the soul by educating the mind.

Shadow of a Man

In the shadow of a man with initials MLK,
in the shadow of a man using X as his name,
in the shadow of men who take responsibility for their domain,
young boys make babies as a claim to fame.
young girls easily succumb to the charmers' game.

At your young age, educating your mind
not procreating your kind is proof of your ability to shine.
Babies need intelligent parents not "please take a number and
wait in line".

Although your surroundings may pull you down,
there is one sure way to get off the ground.
By learning the three "R's",
you will improve the future for those you conceive
and create a society that continually achieves.

Believe in yourself and you shall never go wrong;
only through education and knowledge will you truly become strong.
For knowledge is power and power is strength
and strength gives you the courage to go to any length.

A shadow is created by the absence of light,
but, to cast a shadow, one must first stand in the light.

Beside the shadow of a man is the shadow of a woman,
working together, they properly can shape
the growth and the pattern their family should take
and when the time is right, they will produce rainbows of might
who use intelligence not ignorance as their shadows of light.

Open Your Mind

If I were a spirit
embodied in your mind,
could I open a window
to enlighten your kind?

Could I look upon your face
without pity and disgrace
while introspective tears
continue salting the
wounds of my race?

Haiku

when the last leaf fell
strangers cut all signs of life
from the hollow tree

Haiku For My Queen

My Queen was happy
until they tore her children
from her weary arms

My Queen wept deeply
while traitors sold her treasures
from the river Nile

My Queen danced no more
when her prince and princess sailed
to the western worlds

Fruit of My Hand

Bitter-sweet is the fruit you placed in my hand,
Shedding not desired, of my melanin tan,
Closing is my mind since stolen from my land.

Barren is your mind, as a field tainted by toxic flow,
Frozen is your heart, as the welcome of an ageless whore,
Sinking is my spirit since I have nothing with which to row,
You handed me an anchor instead of a life-saving oar.

Bitter-sweet is the fruit you now eat from my hand,
Obsessive is your desire to match my beautiful tan,
Fewer are the closing doors that slowly destroy our land.

Golden is the lining of the clouds only I can see,
Reddening is your neck since you fear the shifting tide,
A tide changing exclusive terms to words like us and we,
Equality and dignity are the anchors now I ride.

What Time Is It?

Is it time to go or time to stay,
time to work or time to play?
Time to relive your history of racial walls
or rewrite my future's rise without your fall.
Time to relive my history at your beck and call
or rewrite your future to meet equality's calls.
Time to relive our history as a divided past
or rewrite our future as a united cast.

Living the Dream

What does it mean to live the dream?

Do I strive for equality throughout mankind
or oppose the injustice levied upon my line?

Do I challenge the irrational belief of genetic superiority
or struggle to defeat the stereotypes sustained by my own minority?

How do I live the dream
when nightmares still lurk in the shadow of my history?

How do I live the dream
when wrong is right solely due to might?

How do I live the dream when
there is no time to learn that the distant stars are not just a gleam?

I live the dream by deciding that each day the dream shall live through me.

Fading Rights

Listen America, it's time to come down,
get off the high horse and walk on the ground.
Listen to the hypocrisy in your wavering voice,
when you speak of equality and freedom of choice.
Burning the Flag or burning a cross
is freedom of speech and no personal loss
but talking about shooting a cop or praying in school
is a violation of democracy's basic rule.

As you preach religious freedom and national pride,
remember your founding, so no one must hide.
How many lessons will it take you to learn
that freedom is a right not a privilege to earn?
Our privileges earned from rights deserved
and the sovereignty our common blood preserved.

Listen America, open your ears,
to your children's shedding tears.
Listen to the cries in the darkness of the night
as you hesitate performing what you know is right.
How much longer can you delay?
How much more must your children pay?

A Time to Rest

Roll Call

When all is done and said
we stand before our Head,
confessing life as led,
and witness what we said.

The stories we must share
are filled with human err,
a pain we all must bare
for in God we trust and share.

If our conscience is truly clear,
our souls are cleansed of fear
as we kneel and shed a tear
before the angels cheer.

When all is done and said
our life's book completely read
the bread of life, our soul is fed
then we're accepted by the Head.

Angel in Your Heart

Listen Mother to the words I say,
hear the voice that's gone away,
The time we shared, a blessing light,
I sensed your presence day and night,
Your heartbeat rocking me to sleep,
your voice, its melody ever sweet.

For a time, no words shall ease your pain,
neither cards nor flowers remove the strain.
I feel your pain; it does not hide,
I know the burden wells inside.
You feel betrayed; it surrounds,
the guilt within, knows no bounds.

I watch your sadness; I have your eyes,
I know your sadness; I hear your cries,
My journey seemed so well planned,
I too dreamt of holding hands,
God knew the goodness that two created;
a special beauty for which He waited.

Some things are beyond your control
and my ascent was one of those.
He needed an angel to share in His reign
and brighten the radiance of His domain.
Someday as a Guardian, I am to return
and watch over my brother as he grows and learns.

Christian was to be my name,
one of hope now one of pain.
Untroubled times was not His claim,
Not always sunshine not always rain,
I am the miracle for a time you gained;
alive in your heart where our Savior sustains.

Middle of the Night

In the middle of the night I wake wondering
why my lips taste of brine,

then I realize, I still mourn the death of my parents
and the rage of loneliness fills my heart with sorrow
knowing I must wait another day for eternal rest.

Is patience the virtue of a broken heart or
the prize of being faithful?

Tomorrow I will not mourn, I will miss them.

Forever in the Heart

Gentle Wonder spoke humbly when asking to return to the safety of her Master's hands, "I am prepared for this journey that will enlighten all my dreams and quiet the thunder in my head..."
****
Master; do not harshly judge my rushing to Your hands.
My needs were urgent, so I thought, and I dismissed
Your openness to my thoughts.

Enslaved in tattered body, I sought release, I felt so unworthy;
my compassion as seen by others was blind to my eyes,

As you touched my face all knowledge was revealed,
I understood the harshness of my decision
and the forgiveness in Your hands.

Each day I face the anguish of relinquishing earth's domain;
those left behind still weigh heavy on my mind.

Now I sit with you, my pain in full remission, enjoying a few old
friends and accepting life renewed; yet something still is missing;
an emptiness, a void inside of me.

I did not fully grasp the importance of human touch until my family,
I only saw, and could not soothe their anguish of my decision.

Of the many things learned since I journeyed back, one emerges
above the rest, my understanding that family love is forever
and no distance can diminish.
****
My daughter, now you see, the pain you freed left us lonely and void of thee. Rest in quiet slumber until reunited we become and remember that our love is forever, never distance torn apart.

In The Darkness of the Mind

In the darkness of the mind,
we shall never find,
the reason why those we love
too quickly seem to go.

The reason never clearly understood,
Your Love, the message that eludes.

The darkness of the mind cannot comfort those left behind,
we must seek Your Light to find the relief from lonely nights.

In the darkness of the mind,
not solace or shelter shall we find,
we must light the caverns of the mind
and break the chains that darkness binds.

The chains that bind can be broken
by seeking answers outside
the solemn chamber of self-pity thought.

The darkness of the mind shelters nothing we need to find,
only through open minds shall we see Your Plan's Design.

By walking in the light,
we begin to understand that those we love found a better home,
a place of honor in Your Sight where they shall never feel alone.

From Above

Evening Prayer

Each night, I find a quiet space within to reflect on my day.
This evening is not different from many others, except I want to say,
"Thank you Father for watching over and graciously guiding me today".

Praying Hands

With these hands, the world created, life preserved,
judgment passed, comfort and consolation given,
I formed the hearts of those before and those yet to come.

My hands bore the pain of iron spikes driven home to silence love
too vocal for the untrained to hear, too quiet to overlook,
and too tame for the warrior's lance to diminish.

My hands bear the sorrows of a world too young to comprehend
the sacrifice given to expunge the wretchedness of its inhumanity,
and save the many whose feet these hands may never wash.

With these hands I pray that someday you will understand
and gather before the majesty of your soul
and touch thy neighbor's face with the same fullness of life
that fills your heart each time you feel my touch.

*Because I never understood the limits of my brightness,
I became the stars and now I shine.*

Evening Star

Every evening, as I stepped from the shadows of my day,
the stars graced my soul and dressed my wounds.
As their light shone on my face,
I prayed that one day I would touch them
and know their energy.

As I listened to the quiet, His smile engulfed me
and He spoke, "As My Child, you were born a star.
Today, I chose to reveal you to the world.
Go forth with strength and humility;
enlighten with knowledge, understanding and compassion.
Today you shine."

My Best Friend

As life began, me cradle-bound;
this face of smiles became my friend.
When I was hungry or maybe cold,
in her arms she would hold.
I'd fall down and scrape a knee;
she'd be there to comfort me.

Through her eyes I learned the world,
my problems both large and small
became less heavy when she I called.

Time passed on, our roles reversed,
I cared for her as she had for me;
my best friend was leaving me.

Today she's gone; my mother best,
now at peace, now at rest,
I raise my head to praise the Lord
and see someone at His right hand.
My smile grows wider as once again,
I'm looking up at my best friend.

Forgive Me, Please

Please forgive me for my indiscretion,
I became blinded by the glamour, caught up in the fame,
I forgot the purpose of my words, to share the gift you gave.

Another chance I plead, I felt the demon pass,
any punishment well deserved, any forgiveness blind.
The veil lifted from my eyes, the fog cleared from my mind.
Now, I understand the power that is Thine.

Although the flesh is weak, my error holds no excuse,
I ventured on my own and listened to the deep,
instead of hearing thunders reign, I "prodigaled" again.

Entrusted with a talent too soon considered mine,
never completely realizing the faith you placed in me.
My lesson learned, my pride in check,
Your footsteps now my guide.

From conception, I cared for you, asking only reverence due.
When you felt the need to stray, asking that you pray.

Against All Odds

You never burden with more than I could handle,
no unbearable trouble nor threatening scandal.
Giving what is needed, not always asked,
enough to finish the challenge tasked.

Placing strength at my command,
Faith, Your request not demand.
Many challenges faced on even keel,
after learning, when to take a kneel.

Whether in sorrow, in harm or pain,
you were there, my unwavering cane.
When I sought a goal not on my path,
Your gentle nudge felt on my behalf.

As my shepherd and guiding light,
kept me strong and burning bright.
Allowed my tenure on this earth
so I rejoice in my rebirth.

When my time comes and I depart;
I journey home by rote, by heart.
I ask forgiveness for what I have done
that dishonored me and the Three-in-One.

Then You place upon my head
the healing hands of broken bread,
my dreams, my hopes shall be fulfilled;
Your sacrifice in vain not spilled.

This Cup I Cannot Pass

I look around, I feel too new to apostle the words You ask.
I see all is Thine; I am humbled by Your presence.

I hear Your Words, then look around, something seems amiss.
Your shepherd's staff led me well, guiding me from danger.
Now You ask for a leap of faith to cross my greatest challenge.

I look around and see others straying from Your spoken path.
Do you want me working side-by-side with those unproven to
Your task? What do you mean mine is not to judge but to
follow with an opened heart, a model for Your way?

No, I am not without, first nor last,
I cannot cast a stone.
Your point well taken,
a decision I must make.
I know the answer,
this cup I cannot pass.

Help me please,
which path am I to walk,
against my grain with disdain,
or with your grain and the pain
that comes with righteous living?

I look around, I understand, my mind and spirit now one.
My actions and my words...Your gifts, Your tools, guided by Your Light.

In This Home

In this home, respect, trust and cooperation are the guiding principles. The abundance of patience is the cornerstone of our commitment to God, our guests and each other.

In this home, evil does not enter, "cannot" is left at the curb, and loneliness does not exist; God's grace and understanding thrive in an environment of charity and encouragement.

In this home, challenges are sought as opportunities to succeed. Gratitude, faith and hope nourish the recipes of our desires and vigilant prayer is the bond that secures our future.

The blessings of this home encircle all whom cross its threshold as does the friendship of its caretakers, within these walls expect to always feel the humility of this special place to rest.